Blue Air

Also by Kate Gale

Where Crows & Men Collide, poetry 1995
Water Moccasins, fiction 1994 (as Kate Gale Harper)

Blue Air

Poems

Kate Gale

Red Hen Press

1995

Blue Air

Cover art by Rachel Hobreigh.

Some of these poems have previously appeared in the following periodicals, to whose editors grateful acknowledgement is made: *The Academic Forum, The Village Idiot, Soundings East, Inside English, Westwind Review,* and *Northeast Journal.*

Acknowledgement is also made to Ben Saltman, Marian Olson, and to Angela Ball at the University of Southern Mississippi.

Second Edition
ISBN 0-9639528-5-4
Library of Congress Catalog Card Number 95-070408

Red Hen Press
P.O. Box 304
15333 Sherman Way
Van Nuys, CA 91406

For Mark who will not be forgotten

Table of Contents

Blue Air

Directions for Dreams

She wants a trip to somewhere,
Georgia O'Keefe's New Mexico
to hear the rocks sing
the red and brown song
or Graceland to smell Elvis money.

I bake fresh bread,
smell yeast rising
wipe flour from my palms
rest them on my knees
write poetry from between my teeth.

In this large country, her dreams
wait for directions. She could paint.
Do I know how much writers make?
She could act. Actors'
houses are made of money.

She asks my help to find her dreams. I am on my knees
picking up children's crayons. Who do you think you are?
she asks. Ah, I say, because there are so few
possibilities when talking to the lost,
and I pick up my pen and begin writing.

A Woman Who Wants to Fish

Elissa May kneels in church, lights candles,
prays to a fictitious God for a voyage.
Do you decline, old man? she asks God,
the challenge of opening some window,
I give you until tomorrow, are you ready, old man?
Excuse me, I must go.

It's bizarre how my mother insists I come here.
It's more peculiar how I give in, she thinks,
watching her woman figure in shop windows.
It looks inhuman as if it were a mirage.
She wants to catch a big fish, cook it on the sand.
Maybe, I should wear a mask, but what sort of mask would it be?

She goes to bed to drown in sheets, comes up for air.
She has her own room, but she cannot breathe. She tries
to live like a hermit, but her mother knocks in the morning
to offer bacon. You know my daughter, the mother says,
when introducing Elissa. She shrugs because her daughter
has a few gray hairs in her twenty-five year old uncut locks.

Elissa thinks about juggling and acrobatics. But naturally,
the sea pulls the hardest. She wants to fish. Marry,
her mother tells her, a word, like water, pushing her
toward a narrow dry chute. She pulls guilt like taffy
with her mother who baked yellow cakes
with lavender frosting for her eleventh birthday.

She sleeps lightly, watches the sun rise early and set late.
It tries to pull her over the hill, Good luck, it cries.
She smells dates, smells their foreignness like the body
she lives in with its female odors. She feels desire stirring.
At five she wanted to join the circus, tame lions, ride
elephants. She wanted to be a tiger dreaming tiger dreams.

Her mother knocks. We only have eggs, she says.
When you were a baby, she tells Elissa,
I felt your sharp teeth. Elissa dreams night and day,
but her mother needs her until a man comes
to bring grandchildren, an update to their very old play,
a new scene to the terrifying sameness.

The mother recalls waiting on her wedding night
disguised as wanting, playing out in her head
a private sexual scene, she flew above her wedding bed
in a slow plane. From up there, it looked ridiculous.
Something very important is happening, she told herself.
That night Elissa was conceived.

Elissa lies in her bed at night waiting
for a man or her mother to die. And one comes.
He marries the mother, who at sixty-five,
dyes her grey hair red and leaves with him.
Elissa inherits the house. You can stay here or go fishing,
her mother says, it doesn't matter.

The Face of Christ

The headmaster travels by train, asks God
to show him the face of Christ.
Take a picture out the window,
God says.

In Christian boarding school
the teachers say every day, look at that picture.
If you are clean inside, if you are right with God,
you will see the face of Christ.

I look every day. It is shadows on snow.
Go to the corner, sit by yourself until you see.
The other girls see God; they stand adoring.
I see black and white patches? continents?

They say, this is rebellion. You're going
to start skipping meals. Forgive me, I pray
for my flesh is weak. I see it, I see it,
the face of Christ. Thank you Jesus.

I can walk in the breakfast line.
The other girls give me knowing smiles.

Disappearing Tails

We collect frogs' eggs in gallon jars,
watch them yellow and green in the sun,
hatch wriggly black tadpoles.
One boy eats them on a dare,
swallows four tadpoles, heads and tails.
We listen for frogs croaking in his belly.
He encourages girls to lie on his stomach listening,
asks us to walk in the woods.
He wants to show us something.
I hang back, watch my tadpoles hatching.
The other girls have seen enough.
Their pollywogs are losing tails.
They follow him to a woods place
near the meeting of two streams
where he says grownups never go.
The girls come back red-faced and laughing.
I watch my tadpoles emerge from eggs.

He Said, Talk to Me in Spanish

When I leave Richmond, a ribbon
of dampness on the Eastern part
of my map and drive across
the sandy creases of the middle,
across Texas, I find Arizona.

Paddling through college,
I find a boy, who says, I love you,
takes me here and there, money squeezed
in his pockets. We are the same person,
squeezers of money.

We leave our cages in the morning,
see the world our orchard,
cultivate our minds,
our apple trees,
sell apples for a squeeze of money.

Our parents do not put paper
money in our hands behind our backs
a call us Joseph.
We are the other brothers,
he and I.

His name is Steve Garcia.
He says, talk to me in Spanish.
My friends ask if I know he's Mexican,
and I admit he never told me.
Is he?

Where I come from,
there are no Mexicans. How exotic,
a Mexican, and they look at me
through the doorway, but I cannot see
what they see through their eyes.

Mother Troubles

I have trouble remembering my mother.
Your own mother? You poor thing.
How long has it been?
Ten years.

I have trouble remembering the raised veins in her hands,
how she rubbed away many headaches. Lying in her lap,
I could see her face from below, jaw jutting into a V.
I lay on her lap, her fingers in my forehead.

I don't remember what she said last I saw her, not much.
She was busy, said, I have to go back to work, put her hands
in her grey hair, said she liked the last picture I sent
I looked more natural. I can't make out what you're saying.

I didn't love her. I don't think she ever loved me. I remember
little of our visits. Before I left, she pressed my head
between her breasts where secrets kept, whispered,
"Do not forget me." I don't know what she could mean by that.

I am blank on the subject of my mother.
It is impossible for me to remember anything about her
without remembering her hands on my forehead
in her hair, with raised veins protecting her blood.

Stories that Need to be Told

Those stories ended with marriage and they lived happily,
I wanted to know, what else? because she hadn't done anything
but be the stage on which he acted out his adventures,
catching the princess, winning, wooing.

Surely it couldn't go on like this. Surely she would
take her place as actor and not continue as part of the
floorboards and furniture. But that was the desperate truth,
she was to be who? the gal who's married to so-and-so.

And even after the feminists turned the page, babies
kept clinging to their mothers, and the La Leche League
kept insisting women should stay home with their kids
for twenty years and then rejoin the work force.

There are women who weave rugs, paint pictures
of Los Angeles toppling into the Pacific,
write poems in which Central American women
pick soft ripe fruit on days when there is no artillery fire.

But these women, who are they, where are they?
Why aren't their stories being told?
Because I'd like to know, if I have to be a woman,
what happened ever after?

About Peaches

He wears blue jeans, a plaid shirt, smells of grease
and after shave. She picks the hard dry peaches that fall
out of season. The wind is cold. She wears her resistance lightly
like her worn cotton shorts and shirt.

She wants college in the fall. He wants babies
in the springtime. She saves money at the bank
and goes across the street to the thrift store.
She kisses him in his car on Saturdays.

He takes her to Burger joints and parties
where his friends drink beer. She hugs her knees
and looks at the stars. It is a warm summer. She smells
ripe peaches on the wind. She has decided to be a doctor.

Their kisses become wetter. He takes her hand
and says, here's a lesson in anatomy.
His laugh grinds over her, stops the flow of wanting
that edged her toward him on the seat.

He starts again under a full moon, patient, hungry,
his breath in her ears. He dips his face
in the V of her legs and comes up smiling and wet
like a dog from a stream, and she has lost her mind now.

She can't remember how it all happens. It's okay, only
she wishes they could have talked first. Her brain feels
left out. Her body and his conspired alone. The ripe peaches
she'd brought squish beneath them and juice runs down the seat.

Instead of Kissing

We rake leaves and burn them.
scrape fungi from old logs,
the size of a hand,
write on them,
my name, your name.
We name the tree, the "Shininin Tree."
Skin scrapes off our legs
as we climb, dive
into brackish cold pools,
come up in beavers' houses.
Night settles
around us
sitting on rocks,
slipping in quietly
as trout, one last time, looking
up through stream water,
through night air,
we see the moon shining
down to touch
creatures in shadows.
We hold hands
under water,
rise to the surface,
part, climb out
alone,
hurry into clothes
and through woods
in separate silence.

The Invisible Woman

The invisible woman cries soundlessly,
smell her lasagna, see her breath,
feel her beneath you in silence.

My mother lifted herself around me.
Her fingers to her lips spelled silence.
She taught me pillow tears.

Finally, she stopped
speaking at all, hoping
I would learn invisibility by example.

Red Salamander

"Thou shalt not suffer a witch to live."
I raise a cautious hand, "What's a witch?"
"What do you think?" he looks over his glasses
to see who interrupts the flow of God.
"A witch is a story? like the witch
that wants to eat you in Hansel and Gretel?"

"A witch is a woman who practices the occult, or reads
horoscopes, or talks to animals," he says, and continues
to read who else God will not suffer to live.
I walk on dead leaves through woods touching
oak and maple trees. "Occult, horoscope," I say,
mouthing unfamiliar words like candy.

I almost step on a red salamander
walking on wet earth toward clear water.
"How are you today, Mr. Salamander?"
I pick him up on leaves.
I've heard he likes his skin kept cool.
I don't want to warm him with my fingers.

"Mr. Salamander,"
I look in his beady eyes, his tail flickers,
his whole body twists like rubber.
I put him down, lean into a tree
to watch him slither away.
I look around, did anyone hear?

Shoes and Poetry

Every day I measure by lists,
today mine says shoes and poetry.
Perhaps a poem will come
from God or a shoe salesperson.
All God's children got shoes.
Barefooted, I begged God to adopt me,
but he was busy, like the old woman
in the shoe. The problem with God
I figured out later is that
the earth is overpopulated.
It's mind boggling for God.
He wants to help,
but there are too many of us.
He'd like us to write
our own poems, kids
quit asking for shoes,
do I look like Santa Claus?
But on this hungry planet,
sometimes, we have no one else to ask.

Boarding School Farewell

I do not speak or cry.
I hold on to silence.
A primal howl erupts
from the back of the truck
where we crowd together.
Some children hold hands; some whimper.
The howler kneels, looks through slats
at the disappearing house.
Mommy! he is not tall enough
to see over the back.
Our parents wave at our tears,
turning backs on outstretched hands.
I shut my mouth as tight as my teddy bear.

Saying Yes

The thing I don't like, is having to--anything.
At first I had to, because at three,
it's hard to run away from home.
At eighteen I ran, showing them my back,
a flat no.

I had to keep turning that flat no
to most things, school because of time,
food because of fat, cars because of noise,
men because of sex, sex because of men.
I wrote my way in and out of darkness,

climbed streets, said yes, and grey light,
the reflection of shadows,
turned colors as I walked
through tears I'd held back
and salvaged in every other life.

Molasses and Honey

I must have been small. The molasses was even with my eyes
across the table, blackstrap molasses for toast.
Beside it, honey. The molasses is thick and bitter.
Which would you like, she asks.
I can't see into the honey bowl. I say, Molasses.
She usually gives, what I don't want.

She pours the thick black liquid with hairy hands,
eats honey herself. All the grownups eat honey.
I crunch my toast, staining my small fingers.
Now I sit cross legged, gathering my husband,
my children, my books, but I do not speak as we eat
our toast and honey.

Someone with hairy hands waits to pull
the honey bowl away, to pour molasses on my bread.
Some days, those hairy hands are all around me.

Orange Windows

There used to be a little window.
Out of it I saw the sea
clapping for its own music.
Leaves of a maple tree fluttered down,
orange. I pressed them beneath
wax paper. I lay sick.

Now the sun filters through smog,
never reaches me. My house is K-mart curtains.
I start my novel the eighteenth time
to please him.
I drink orange-spice tea.
My sunset swirls in a teacup.
There is no sea.

My Father and Food

My Father and I
do not need each other.
I have a husband,
he has a wife.
I carry a baby
who will never say grandpa.

I met him twice,
the first it was snowing.
I was anxious and dripped
ketchup from my French fries.
He studied me like
leftovers.

Two years later when I called
he said he had no time
to read my letters,
said I'd seemed fat
when he met me.
I said, "Ah."

The second time was hot,
Philadelphia steamed.
I was California
blond, tanned,
had a plane to catch.
Over chicken salad,

I crumbled out my life for him;
he gave me only select slices of his.

Squirrel Life

I'm coming home late, crushed by darkness,
my mind, hobbled by freeways, the overpasses
stacked like smashed cars being hauled away.
My hands fidget on the wheel. I'm busy
running across wires for nuts, running home
to husband, house, children. I drive.

All this flashes through me and the car,
a ribbon on Los Angeles streets.
There's a man ahead carrying something,
a bag of earth, I think, glancing at the road,
back at the man, and the thing I see is alive,
climbing the man's body like a goblin, a monkey?

All those flashes tumbling through me like water,
and I see then, a child on his father's back.

Signs and Flying

The sign by the road lets go
of its posts, floats upward.
I grip the steering wheel.
The wheels of the car grab
the road, give up on flying or never
wanted to. I have always wanted to fly,
not like birds, more like white
angels speaking the words of God.
I speak words that cling
to pavement.
I want them to float like spider webs.
Webs connecting us.
I say to you, yes, and you say, yes,
and the breath of our yeses
spins gold through pale air.

Green Rain

I drive all day in rain. Fog lifts.
I see everything green. Yesterday
you touched me for the first time,
your arm on my shoulders. I felt it,
like a lover you wait for. We need this rain
after the long drought. You kissed my cheek,
said you loved me. I reached
out my arms but couldn't speak.
Like the girl in the songs of Solomon
I cried, "I will run after you."
You discovered me late in life.
You hold me like a new baby. I look
up at you. The rain keeps falling.
Have you noticed how green everything is?

My New Wallet

The new leather wallet he gave me for Mother's Day
holds two crisp one dollar bills rubbing faces
to backs for warmth, for ecstasy. They don't want
to leave my wallet which feels like silk,
an empty womb waiting to be fertilized.
The dollars refuse to multiply.
They hold clammy hands to a fire
like two bums, but other bums don't crowd near.
Under an ugly sky, they huddle together.
Why is it always just us? they say.

I am Red

You say, what's wrong with you?
I'm telling you. I'm red.
We who are red have run away
from well-ordered households
with napkin holders and curtains.

At parties, where women nod over wine coolers,
My boredom bristles like porcupine quills.
I stare into each set of eyes. I see the large whites.
They become white people.
They extend hands and say, how are you?

They hope desperately I will say something normal.
They can see my skin is dangerous.
It wants to be free.
They squint.
They walk away from me.

From the Bible to Poetry

I walked between the Bible's thin pages,
stepped out like the truth from a liar's mouth.
I scrambled to a rock where I hear
my own voice, muddled by echoes.

I turn myself around. I turn
from that white wall, from black
marching orders on thin paper.
I get out of line and run

to a bookstore, where poetry flies
toward real life, and swallows it,
spitting out a new world on pages
where lines are not even symmetric.

Puddle Face

In rain, I hear voices. I cup it,
dip my face in it, my eyes soggy
with water, my lashes dripping like
sodden petals. I try to see where
I am going, or where someone else is going
so I can know whether to follow.

Where do I want to go? You have to ask?
I want to go to heaven. It seems simple,
like the act of picking up pen,
and scratching on paper
to gain immortality,
like the simple act of kissing.

We lean over a puddle, see ourselves
in a basin of mud which holds us up to the sky.
Where are we going? Hello there;
the puddle face stays with me.
Where are we going?
Hello there.

The Doorway of Secrets

Something follows me, a dog or my shadow.
It haunts me on quiet days
in the thick of woods
like a bear or a mountain lion stalking me.
It leans toward me, fuzzes the edges of thoughts.

It stays there, just out of reach,
a maddening itch my arms are too stiff to touch.
I stare in the mirror hoping to see a trace of it
between my eyes or written on my forehead.
But my forehead is a shelf of closed books.

I close my eyes for a moment. For a moment
I am in the doorway of secrets; but I do not knock.
I fold my arms across my chest and turn away because in there,
I think, is a bloated, frenzied squaw,
kneeling, bending, wheedling, covering old sores.

Damaged Woman

A man says to me over dinner
if you would suggest it, we would go.
I touch my lips which have all the power in the room
to say, "let's go," but they wait for my brain
which lies tangled in the kelp of morals,
loyalties, vows, rigidity.

My lips rarely consult the body in these matters.
They assume the brain will take precedent.
I eat melted cheese on chips,
running into arteries, packing thighs.
My lips consult my body which yawns
open for fat and sugar.

My brain whispers, "No," but the belly is firm,
"You shut up," the obedient lips open and close.
The man watches, his whole body in prayer.
He wonders if he could re-connect
some missing wire or whether
the woman is irreparably damaged.

Betsey and Marigold

Renoir women with their large sloping bellies
white legs and bosoms, loll on couches
in my dreams. They have names
like Betsey and Marigold.

Betsey says, "look at these darling
little stick creatures." "Darling?"
Marigold's lips curl. She eats passion fruit,
has red hair. "They're pitiful."

We twentieth century creatures suggest
Betsey and Marigold go to Weight Watchers,
Jenny Craig, Nutra System. There are
options for women in your condition.

They invite children into awesome laps,
suckle babies from breasts that could feed
the planet, invite lovers
to rush into rounded thighs.

We run, we stick our hated bodies
into size 8 or 6, 4 if we're lucky.
We watch over our shoulders, afraid the scale
will find a voice, "She's gaining, she's gaining."

We sit at the table, knees together, stomachs flat,
bosoms bound, careful faces arranged
like a table for two.
Betsey and Marigold roar with laughter.

Isaac and Rebecca

And he said to her, let down, I pray you,
thy pitcher and give me to drink. And Rebecca
said, I will get thee drink and thy camels also.

I see this woman kneel in wet earth, her pitcher deep
in the well, pouring out water that slides into the man
like life, sweat on her neck like slime.

The man tells her father, I want this woman,
to be my master Isaac's wife. Her father says, "Go,"
and she says, "Yes." "Yes" as she rides off in darkness.

"Yes," many days later, in a strange city.
A strange man, Isaac, lifts her down, smiles
until his teeth show. She follows him to his tent,

lies down where he tells her,
says, my God. He gives her the blood of grapes
spilling down breasts and belly, into hard earth.

A World Without God

He told me, never say it's impossible,
rubbing the back of my neck,
nothing's impossible,
kissing the back of my hand,
leather close enough for me to smell
putting down his keys.
I've promised God, I say.
He doesn't stop breathing.
He moves behind me, reaching
for the buttons
of my green dress.
I get up, say goodbye, the word
hanging between us, an icicle
from eaves.
His eyes, my eyes,
stay linked. We move
together. I walk
backward, my hands behind me;
he walks forward
both arms outstretched. I trip;
we fall forward together
into some other world
where there is no God.

From Guatemala, to this House

The woman has marks of violence and love.
She thinks she is pregnant.
She returns to our house
freshly slapped, freshly painted.
Outside she stands by the trees,
watering them, talking to herself, muttering.

At thirteen, she married. She screeches now
like an owl who never found its voice.
She left because her husband beat her,
but says he misses her now.
We go to the north country,
to collect acorns and pinecones.

She lived in a hut with the crows,
but misses the dark blooms of her home.
In her dreams, someone bites her chin,
bruises her child's head.
She sweats and remembers
how her husband hated female odors.

He'd stay with his brother during her time of month.
He'd love her with daily American showers.
She mounts the motorcycle behind her boyfriend.
It reminds her of the trip from her country,
unfamiliar transportation, unfamiliar shapes
between her legs. She holds on.

The baby laughs. She listens with eyes closed.
She shifts, changes every day.
She wants to return. She wants to stay.
She is pregnant; something snakes up inside her
to get rid of it before it dances in her belly.
She crosses herself. She cuts off her hair.

Sex and Rainbows

I expected to be raised to some point
where drugs take you, my soul swimming
higher like a salmon leaping
upstream, flashing in sunlight,
pink water diamonds around me, unaware
of the conscious world, my body an instinct.

In a dark room, I shed my clothes
like a prisoner for inspection. He
shed his clothes like a boxer
in the ring. My head down
waiting for approval,
his head up, waiting for everything.

When I started melting,
it wasn't a dream.
It was a deliberate male act.
I dropped to my knees and slipped down,
his hands roaming my body
like the Gauls plundered Europe.

I could still speak,
my world, my world, my beautiful
world, as the shining rainbow of a salmon
twisting upward blackened,
and I opened my eyes. I never
expected anything this big.

Gods and Spiders

I scream, falling into
shallow water up there on stage.
I try not to laugh,
thinking how you'd
float across those boards
smoothly like Christ.

Reincarnation runs in cycles.
You were a general, a queen bee,
a dark night, an Olympic winner.
I was a bug, a night crawler,
a spider's web, a movie screen.
You were a Himalayan god.

Two Women

My husband once slept with two women.
One was a Jew, the other a Gentile.
The Jew had children. Her vagina gripped him
tightly, a child-bearing vise. Directly he slipped
to the Gentile lawyer. She breathed money in his ear.
Sometimes I'm afraid the sun will rise
too early, dry up the dew on my grass.

That Gentile had tiny bones. One is careful
with fragile people. I am an oak tree.
She held him with curved legs. I breathe homework.
I do not sing. He reminds me of this.
The sun is coming, and I am a star,
or want to be one, I climbed a hill
and now I see my path is bones.

Did you know men can fantasize
every pubic mound they ever saw?
Maybe if I could walk
a row of penises,
handle every one,
I'd walk on between the elms,
and know I'd come home.

Fights

Words cross, mine going north,
his flying south; is this a fight?
We never hit each other.
I chill, look out the window
at the magnolias in blossom.
The sun is going down.
In other parts of the world
it is rising.

Lauretta

1.

You saw me across a crowded room, recognized
your pinnacle of womanhood in my bowed head,
faltering step, stammered, "I'm sorry",
while a man spilled wine on my neck and breasts.
You came to me, adored my yellow dress over many Coronas.
I lapped compliments from the floor around your feet,
licking them from your boots, running off the porch,
eating one out of the dirt. I licked my way into your life.
You said, I love you, on cue, like an actor.
I trembled at those words and dropped limp.

2.

We ride out of town,
my horse trailing yours, nose to tail.
You are wanted for murder
of a girl with a throaty laugh.
Her bones clickety clack all day.
I ride behind you, cook stew, water horses, rub you down.
You're an angel, you say.
I want my angel title,
keep doing angel things, become more transparent daily.
I hold up my hands and see skirts through them.

3.

You walk over hills like John Wayne.
I crawl from window to window
looking out at a world too bright for my eyes.
I hear you talk about your old lady
in the kitchen, the bedroom,
your voice caving in around me,
until in the cave,
there is just your voice, my head,
your voice in my head,
and my bones going clickety-clack.

House of Anger

Balance this, you say,
pointing at columns of figures that won't match.
But I have slept peacefully
through years of unbalanced checkbooks.

Your anger fills our house. It explodes the windows,
moves out into the lawn. It becomes a house
moving toward me, stepping on its foundations,
wading through earth.

You have your own faults, you say.
I am full of holes like a rebel under fire,
and that is why I stay, leaning against the wall,
gathering silence around me like a blanket.

But I do not have to tell you this.
You have seen me standing here.

Dry Sandwiches

He cuts his sandwich, gives half to me.
Eat it. Between neat moustache
and white face, handsome
as a statue, his mouth moving.
His words slide around the table.
I am a poet from Columbia University.

I sip tea in the small box of air
around my head. He rubs soft hands.
I don't want
to discuss poetry with a beautiful woman.
I want to enjoy the woman.
I taste the wretched dry sandwich.

My poems sit in their folder,
legs closed like young girls
who do not know what they are doing.
Please, I say, I must go.
But he hopes to see me again.
So we can talk more.

He expects me to call, so he can talk
more to a beautiful woman.
I am not. I am squeezed
between the yellow covers
of the folder.
I am silent.

Cactus Dreams

I do not know what makes cactii
rise in the desert,
their insides wet, like my dreams
coming from nowhere.

I rise from the floor of oceans
damp, curved as the neck of a sea horse.
Irises fall from my hair.
My skirt splits to the waist.

I am not a cactus,
not a sweet nothing on your pillow.
I am light curtains blowing
across your face tonight.

Other Children

When I ask about their lives,
my students write of other children.
They say, we waited alone in dark
living rooms. We locked the doors
as we were told. Shows we didn't care
about and can't remember flickered
like blue-light specials while we waited.
Our parents opened doors and closed them
like visitors to a jail. We knew
they were tired. We didn't speak.
We watched perfect tv families
and ate tv dinners until bed.

Other children smile while their mothers
cook meat and vegetables.
They sit around the table
like petals of daisies.
They talk and listen and eat pies.
The other children's parents kiss.
If I could live
on television, I think....
I ask my Mom why we
don't talk; she says, okay, talk,
but I can't remember
what the other children say.

A Question of Work

The question I ask
when they offer more work
is whether I can think
any love colored thoughts
in this classroom,
whether plums are squeezed
until their yellow flesh
grinds to the floor and walls.

I wanted to give,
they wanted to take,
but they never let me out.
From a pool, I could have
returned ready.
One girl tells me
I want you
to talk more.

She throws my head
around the room.
These people cross
their arms and legs.
My arms spread out
on either side of me.
My palms and feet beg
for release.

The Orange Slide

Mark and his son sift sand
in the red and blue playground
behind the orange slide.
Mark's son builds a mound
with his toy shovel.
Mark falls and his son laughs
"Daddy", into his white face.
Mark sits up in the cold Febuary air.

April last year, his son's birthday, this park;
those pizza kite days grow smaller, as if
through the wrong end of a telescope.
Mark is 27, his son almost three.
They go down the orange slide fast,
riding into the dirt. They hit bottom.
The son laughs, but Mark doesn't speak.
He is stunned for a moment to remember where he is.

For Mark

You lie on sheets between pale yellow air
and some other place.
I have kissed you, I have threaded
your life with mine, held your wife's hands,
washed your son's face.

We never believed it would end
with your sweet handsome face
fallen away into the pillow,
your last smiles
sucked out of you.

We are left
with your skin and bones
and the faintest bit of you,
pushing through your lungs,
in and out.

Blue Air

Standing on cool brick steps 5 A.M.
the morning after, still clutching
Mark's face and breath, I watch
the grey blue sky, hunt for reasons.
The newly trimmed palm tree
sways in blue air.

Wind sifts its top where a crow lands in new green.
Mark, I don't know if I told you I loved you.
Palm heart pulses beneath my fingers.
I touch my neck, feel fluttering, lie down
in discards that covered the palm tree yesterday,
my skin dry as leaves.

An airplane's smoke trail slices the sky,
and then I see, what I didn't see;
it's a seam, holding together
the two halves of the sky,
like the middle of a butterfly
or the body of an angel.

Lemon Belly

I lie on the table gripped by hands,
squeezing my belly like a lemon.
Juice drips while I flatten
and scream like a witch in water
without power to say stop
only for a minute,
let me lie down, let me get up,
let me sleep, let me lie awake,
let go of me, you, you,
and I am caught again
by the grinder, until,
like a rag doll,
I am thrown away,
and she nudges from between my legs,
tiny body flows out,
burning fire fingers touch me
raw, naked, whimpering.
Her blue eyes open
to blot out the hours
in the vice.
She nuzzles for milk
like a kitten.
I can hold this kitten
in both hands.
I can say,
I made this,
like a chicken
with her egg.
I can walk around her clucking.

My Bonsai Tree

my bonsai tree I bought at the nursery
the man said to clip it shape it with scissors
but I never shape the tree
I like shapeless skirts and blouses to hide
everything I hide myself
the bonsai tree in the window stretches
branches out and out I am not
afraid under my clothes I walk
by my daughter who runs naked
through the house naked
onto the patio she wilds around
our yard banking turns left and right
until my husband yells put a leash on her
and I turn in my shapeless cloth habit
like a nun in line I turn toward him
stretching arms that are just learning
to move turning
like a blind woman toward the sun
I say I know as she torrents past us
in a wave of flying baby girl
like I never ran like I never laughed
I marched in rigid black lines
with my eyes straight ahead clipetty clip
my shoulders square left right
my back poker straight left left
I will not cut my bonsai tree
Wheee she screams
Wheeeeeeeeeee!

Morning Dolphins

Blue hands white fingers caress
the breast of sand.
Grey fog kisses hands.

In this scene of the movie of my life, first take, last take
I am small, drifting down sand, responsibility
fingers pulling me everywhere.

Swimming parallel to me, six dolphins
rise and plunge, their grey backs sloping up
into the fog, then down to their real life.

I walk unsure whether the dolphins follow me
or I follow them, I feel the kiss of fog,
I wait for voices, is this scene silent?

We dive deep, on all sides the colors of the birth of life
the greens, the blues, melt into us, we feel
our present world and are satisfied.

After the Reading

We tilt forward, fall into each other.
I catch your eyes in my hands,
stand there holding part of you I've never seen;
your colors painted with broad brushstrokes by a good painter.
We tip into each other, kids on a seesaw,
slippery hands holding for balance.
I fall forward, so close to you,
our faces become one.
I almost kiss you.
I almost eat your tongue and lips.
I've been throwing my limbs like a bad dancer,
I want them back.
We stand away from each other, adults,
change our masks like guilty lovers.
Like lovers we arrange our pants and dresses.
We walk away separate.
Bits of you cling to me.